PRAYING THROUGH THE GOSPELS

30 Day Devotional

SARAH MALANOWSKI

Praying Through the Gospels, Second Edition

PUBLISHER: Shine Press
4522 W. Village Dr. #1294 Tampa Florida 34624
Shine-Press.com | Jodi@Shine-Press.com

Cover and book interior design by Sondra Howe

Published in the United States of America
ISBN: 978-1-947066-20-5

1. HEATH & FITNESS / Mental Health
2. RELIGION / Christian Living / Spiritual Growth 15.01.09

ENDORSEMENT
Praying through the Gospels

Diving straight to the heart of the Gospel message, Sarah shows us beautifully how to take Scripture to a place of deeply personal prayer in our own lives. Bring on the hunger and thirst for God's righteousness so that we can be in such a posture of intimate prayer before our Creator! Be prepared to draw closer to the One who loves you so!

—SANDRA LOVE MALANOWSKI
Chick-Fil-A Marketing (Retired)

DEDICATION

This book is humbly dedicated to my Savior and King, my Lord Jesus Christ. Without You and Your sacrifice this book wouldn't be possible! I pray every word in here will honor You.

To my 8th grade girls. Watching you grow and embrace all that God has called you to be is a great joy in my life. I pray that you will be the world changers of tomorrow and that you will always be equipped to walk out a vibrant relationship with Jesus. May these prayers enhance the life you live and continue to bring out the godly characteristics knit in each one of you!

To New Life Students. You embody what I looked for when I was your age. Your passion, love for Jesus, and worshipful hearts are truly inspiring. Thank you for being a source of refreshment to me every Wednesday as I watch you embrace the journey God has for you and bring out the magnificent colors in your circles of influence. You are what this world needs and it is an abundant joy to watch you walk in God's calling on your life!

Blessed are those
who **HUNGER**
and **THIRST** for
righteousness,
for they will be **FILLED.**

(Matthew 5:6)

CONTENTS

Foreword 9
Introduction 11
Day 1: Spiritual Healing 13
Day 2: Influential for Jesus 15
Day 3: Stumbling over My Pride 17
Day 4: Free in Jesus 19
Day 5: Working for the Kingdom 21
Day 6: Light and Salt 23
Day 7: Serving My Lord 25
Day 8: Always Seeking 27
Day 9: Pulling Back the Curtain 29
Day 10: Intrinsic Value 31
Day 11: Living the Abundant Life 33
Day 12: Safe in God's Hands 35
Day 13: For God's Glory 37
Day 14: Living by Faith 39
Day 15: Have Mercy on Me. 41
Day 16: No Comparison. 43
Day 17: Filled with Awe 45
Day 18: A Servant's Heart 47
Day 19: No More Grumbling. 49

Day 20: My Offering 51
Day 21: Pruning Time 53
Day 22: Righteous Anger. 55
Day 23: My Responsibility. 57
Day 24: A Forgiving Heart. 59
Day 25: Holy Spirit Duct Tape. 61
Day 26: Overwhelmed. 63
Day 27: Act of Compassion. 65
Day 28: Forgiveness Matters. 67
Day 29: Jesus Is Risen. 69
Day 30: As I Go 71

Bibliography 73
About the Ministry 75
About the Author 79

FOREWORD

Charles Spurgeon once said, "Never lose heart in the power of the gospel. Do not believe that there exists any man, much less any race of men, for whom the gospel is not fitted." Reading and praying through the words of Jesus found in the four gospels is like taking a walk in the old neighborhood where you grew up. Daily spending time with the inspired words of Matthew, Mark, Luke, and John is like reuniting with your old friends at a high school reunion. It just feels like home!

Sarah Malanowski is not only an experienced writer, but she is also a solid believer, who lives out her faith as a wife, a mother and a friend. Sarah doesn't just give us directions for the journey, she does, as I have seen her do so many times over the years, take us by the hand and walk with us through the journey. For her, writing devotionals is not just to create a collection of books, but the postscript of her daily walk with Jesus.

Praying through the Gospels will help you to not only walk daily in the words of Jesus, but more than that, it will actually get you walking with Jesus. We all have days when we aren't sure where to turn in our Bibles. This book gives us a clear path for the journey. We all have days we don't know how to pray. The daily prayers in this book give you the words to express your heart to the Lord. It is especially helpful on days when you just don't know what to pray or don't feel like praying.

When Jesus said, "Go and make disciples," Sarah Malanowski took Jesus seriously. That is the purpose of this devotional book. Sarah wants to enable you, encourage you, and equip you to be a better follower of Jesus Christ.

—GLEN HOWE
Retired Pastor / Chaplain

Rejoice
in hope,

be PATIENT in
tribulation,

be CONSTANT
in prayer.

Romans 12:12

INTRODUCTION

Has your spiritual heart gone in to cardiac arrest? Has your walk with the Lord become a dull routine? Do you need a little "pick-me-up?"

If yes, then this book is for you. Praying through the Gospels gives you an opportunity to experience Jesus in a fresh way. Take a walk with Jesus through the streets of Jerusalem. Get to know Him and glean from His wisdom.

In your hands, you hold an intimate peak into my own personal journal entries. You will find my heart splashed among the pages of this book. My hope is that these prayers will encourage and inspire you. I promise that you will receive more from this devotional if you take the time to read the passage of scripture mentioned each day.

Some of these prayers might not apply to you, and some might really surprise you. My hope is that through this thirty-day devotional, your personal prayer life will be enhanced with the Lord. I pray that you will glean from God's Word and apply it to your life daily.

I think the best place to start with this book is right where Jesus taught His followers to pray. May you find this simple prayer to be life changing, and may it give you a perfect jump start in to sweet fellowship with the Lord.

> *Pray, therefore, like this: Our Father Who is in heaven, hallowed (kept holy) be Your name. Your kingdom come, Your will be done on earth as it is in heaven. Give us this day our daily bread. And forgive us our debts, as we also have forgiven (left, remitted, and let go of the debts, and have given up resentment against) our debtors. And lead*

(bring) us not into temptation, but deliver us from the evil one. For Yours is the kingdom and the power and the glory forever. Amen.

—MATTHEW 6:9–13 (AMP)

The older I get, the more I realize how much time I need in prayer. The more I mature in Christ, the more I realize it's His work in me that produces anything good. I can't be victorious without recognizing my need for Jesus. My victory in life comes through my humble dependence on the Lord.

I pray that you will experience the victory God has waiting for you through the pages of this book. May these prayers refresh, revive, and reinvigorate your soul. May your spirit find joy in the presence of God. And may you receive a fresh outpouring of God's love through these pages.

Your Sister in Christ,

Day 1

SPIRITUAL HEALING

When they had crossed over, they came to land at Gennesaret. And when the men of that place recognized Him, they sent word into all that surrounding district and brought to Him all who were sick; and they implored Him that they might just touch the fringe of His cloak; and as many as touched it were cured.

—MATTHEW 14:34–36 (NASB)

Pray It Through

Dear Father God, I see that many came to receive physical healing from Jesus but failed to recognize their need for spiritual healing. Lord, I come to You for spiritual healing. I seek You and pray that You will show me where I have gone off track. Please help me to see where my heart has not been pleasing in Your sight. Help me to recognize where my attitude needs to change, and give me the strength to walk every day ahead. Lord, I want so badly to bring You glory, and the greatest way I can do that is to recognize my need for You daily.

Lord, please test me and try me. See if there is any offensive way in me and lead me in the way everlasting (Psalm 139:23–24). I pray that You will create in me a clean heart O God and renew a right spirit within me (Psalm 51:10–12). I am Yours, Lord! I pray that my weakness will only serve to advance Your strength. May Your purpose be what I long for and may my daily steps honor You!

Thank You, Lord, for the power of healing that You provide for my life!

> *If my people, who are called by My name, will humble themselves and pray and seek My face and turn from their wicked ways, then will I hear from heaven and will forgive their sin and will heal their land.*
>
> — 2 CHRONICLES 7:14

Day 2

INFLUENTIAL FOR JESUS

And Jesus said to them, "Watch out and beware of the leaven of the Pharisees and Sadducees." —MATTHEW 16:6 (NASB)

Pray It Through

Lord, I know that it only takes a little yeast to affect a whole batch of dough. The yeast of this world could very easily corrupt me and lead me away from Your truth. I pray that the yeast of this world will not affect the work of You in my life.

Lord, please give me the strength to overcome the influence of this world. I pray that instead of being influenced, I can be influential. May I influence people for You! May I separate myself from the ideas and temptations of this world so that I can influence people to follow You and know You.

Lord, I desire to be a full servant for Your purpose alone. Please help me to recognize the times when I am giving in to the influence of this world. Please help me to remember that my wealth is in You. I'm saving up for eternity. The pleasures of this world cannot satisfy my heart. Please help me to see when I'm allowing the world to dictate what beauty is to me. May I remember that true beauty comes from a heart sold out to You!

If God gives such attention to the appearance of wildflowers—most of which are never even seen—don't you think he'll attend to you, take pride in you, do his best for you? What I'm trying to do here is to get you to relax, to not be so preoccupied with getting, so you can respond to God's giving. People who don't know God and the way he works fuss over these things, but you know both God and how he works. Steep your life in God-reality, God-initiative, God-provisions. Don't worry about missing out. You'll find all your everyday human concerns will be met."

—MATTHEW 6:30–33 (MSG)

Day 3

STUMBLING OVER MY PRIDE

He must become greater, I must become less.

—JOHN 3:30

Pray It Through

Lord, it's really that simple. You must become greater in me, and I must become less. I see how often my pride gets in the way of Your work, and I'm truly sorry for that. I pray that You will help me overcome my pride.

Lord, may I remember that I'm a servant. Here to serve You. Here to do Your will! Here to advance Your purpose. I am not my own. I was bought with a price. You paid the price for my sins. You redeemed me from the pit of hell.

Lord, may I daily live to honor the sacrifice made on my behalf. May I not live to please myself or the desires that I have. But may I live to please You and seek Your desires. Oh God, my king, my refuge, and my strength. I pray that I will remember the truth of John 3:30, "Jesus must become greater in me and I must become less." I live to please You O Lord. I live to bring You praise!

Therefore humble yourselves under the mighty hand of God, that He may exalt you at the proper time.

—1 PETER 5:6 (NASB)

Day 4

FREE IN JESUS

So if the Son sets you free, you will be free indeed.
—JOHN 8:36

Pray It Through

Lord, I desire to crucify this sinful nature that lives in me. I know that I am free because Your Son set me free. I do not have to accept my sinful ways. I can make them submit to You as Your holiness transforms my very being.

For to me, to live is Christ and to die is gain.
—PHILIPPIANS 1:21

Lord, I pray that my life here on this earth will honor You. I pray that each day, I will become closer to You and ever look more like what I see in Your word! I pray that Your word will be alive and active in me.

For though we live in the world, we do not wage war as the world does. The weapons we fight with are not the weapons of the world . . . On the contrary, they have divine power to demolish strongholds. We demolish arguments and every pretension that sets itself up against the knowledge of God, and we take captive every thought to make it obedient to Christ.

—2 CORINTHIANS 10:3–6

Lord, please help me to always remember that I do not wage war the same way the world does. You have given me the spiritual armor (Ephesians 6:10–18) that I need to battle each day. May I stand firm in Your truth and let nothing move me. May I not sway to and fro in the world's opinion, but remain steadfast with my eyes ever fixed on Jesus (Hebrews 12:1–2).

For the word of God is living and active. Sharper than any double-edged sword, it penetrates even to dividing soul and spirit, joints and marrow; it judges the thoughts and attitudes of the heart.

—HEBREWS 4:12

WORKING FOR THE KINGDOM

Then He said to His disciples, "The harvest is plentiful, but the workers are few. Therefore beseech the Lord of the harvest to send out workers into His harvest."

—MATTHEW 9:37–38 (NASB)

Pray It Through

Lord, please increase my compassion for those who are dying in their sins. May my heart break like Yours does, and may I be used to lead people to Jesus. Please give me a greater awareness of those around me who need Jesus, and help me boldly share the good news of salvation. May I be used on a daily basis to advance Your kingdom and Your purpose!

Lord, please give me eyes that see the pain others are facing, ears to listen to those who are hurting, and arms to love those in need. Lord, have all of me, and use me to share the truth of the gospel today!

How beautiful on the mountains are the feet of those who bring good news, who proclaim peace, who bring good tidings, who proclaim salvation, who say to Zion, "Your God reigns!"

—ISAIAH 52:7

Day 6

LIGHT AND SALT

Let me tell you why you are here. You're here to be salt-seasoning that brings out the God-flavors of this earth. If you lose your saltiness, how will people taste godliness? You've lost your usefulness and will end up in the garbage.

Here's another way to put it: You're here to be light, bringing out the God-colors in the world. God is not a secret to be kept. We're going public with this, as public as a city on a hill. If I make you light-bearers, you don't think I'm going to hide you under a bucket, do you? I'm putting you on a light stand. Now that I've put you there on a hilltop, on a light stand—shine! Keep open house; be generous with your lives. By opening up to others, you'll prompt people to open up with God, this generous Father in heaven.

—MATTHEW 5:13–16 (MSG)

Pray It Through

Lord, please help me to never lose my saltiness. I want to bring out the "God flavors" in this world. I want to be used to bring out the flavor of life. I pray that I can be used to show people who You are through my every action. May my actions be pleasing in Your sight. May I be a bringer of joy, peace, and love! May I be used to advance Your kingdom purpose!

Lord Jesus, thank You for being the light of the world and piercing through the darkness. May Your light shine brilliantly through me. May I be used to bring out the "God-colors" in this world.

> *Do you not know that your body is a temple of the Holy Spirit, who is in you, whom you have received from God? You are not your own; you were bought at a price. Therefore honor God with your body.*
>
> —1 CORINTHIANS 6:19–20

Day 7

SERVING MY LORD

But the Lord answered and said to her, "Martha, Martha, you are worried and bothered about so many things; but only one thing is necessary, for Mary has chosen the good part, which shall not be taken away from her."

—LUKE 10:41–42 (NASB)

Pray It Through

Lord, please help me balance my Martha and Mary tendencies. I pray that I will spend more time waiting at Your feet, resting in Your presence, and seeking Your guidance.

> *To be occupied with Christ is more important than to be occupied for Christ. To devote oneself to the Word of Christ, so as to be taught by Him, is more important than to be busy for Him.*
>
> —J. DWIGHT PENTECOST
> *The Words and Works of Jesus Christ*

Lord, I want to spend my time more occupied in Your presence. I want to find myself sitting before You and gleaning from Your word.

I want more of You in my life. Lord, today I pray that I will be more occupied *with* You than *for* You. May I spend more time waiting and less time moving. May I spend more time listening and less time talking. May I spend more time trusting and less time worrying. May I live to serve You today!

> *Each one should use whatever gift he has received to serve others, faithfully administering God's grace in its various forms.*
>
> —1 PETER 4:10

Day 8

ALWAYS SEEKING

So I say to you, Ask and keep on asking and it shall be given you; seek and keep on seeking and you shall find; knock and keep on knocking and the door shall be opened to you. For everyone who asks and keeps on asking receives; and he who seeks and keeps on seeking finds; and to him who knocks and keeps on knocking, the door shall be opened.

—LUKE 11:9–10 (AMP)

Pray It Through

Lord, I see through this that I'm to crave and desire the things of You, to aim and strive for Your best in my life, and to knock at doors of opportunity, not ignore them. When I come to You to ask, seek, and knock, then I will receive, find, and notice the door open to me.

I must step out in faith every day and watch You come through in extraordinary ways. It's a sure thing that You will come through. It's a promise to me, and I cling to it with all my heart.

So today, Lord, I ask to be empowered by Your Holy Spirit. I seek to know Your purpose for my life, and I knock at every door You put before me. May I find many opportunities to glorify You today!

> *O Nebuchadnezzar, we do not need to defend ourselves before you in this matter. If we are thrown into the blazing furnace, the God we serve is able to save us from it, and He will rescue us from your hand, O king. But even if He does not, we want you to know, O king, that we will not serve your gods or worship the image of gold you have set up.*
>
> —DANIEL 3:16–18

What do you find when you look at the throne of your heart? Is God there? Or are your worries, fears, anxieties, children, possessions, and pride there? We all need to take the time to acknowledge what is truly occupying the throne of our hearts. Is it Jesus? If not, something needs to change. Only Jesus deserves the throne. Only He died for our sins that we might live in the freedom God provides.

> *Wait for the LORD; be strong and take heart and wait for the LORD.*
>
> —PSALM 27:14

Day 9

PULLING BACK THE CURTAIN

Under these circumstances, after so many thousands of people had gathered together that they were stepping on one another, He began saying to His disciples first of all, "Beware of the leaven of the Pharisees, which is hypocrisy. But there is nothing covered up that will not be revealed, and hidden that will not be known. Accordingly, whatever you have said in the dark will be heard in the light, and what you have whispered in the inner rooms will be proclaimed upon the housetops.

—LUKE 12:1–3 (NASB)

READ LUKE 12:1-5

Pray It Through

Lord, please show me where I am being hypocritical. Help me to see where I am judging others and need to look more closely at my own sin. Please convict me of my sins quickly and thoroughly and Lord, I pray that I will compare myself to You and no one else. May I not look for the accolades this world can give, but may I quietly live my life surrendered to You and Your purpose.

Lord, I pray that my public life will only mirror what my private life is. May my life reveal a heart in the Word, a steadfast spirit, and a hunger for the things of You. I pray that if someone were to pull back the curtain in my life, all they would see is a life submitted to You.

I pray that if the walls in my home could speak, they would only speak of who You are and the transformation You daily perform in my life. Please help me live a more honorable life before You, O Lord!

Don't pick on people, jump on their failures, criticize their faults—unless, of course, you want the same treatment. That critical spirit has a way of boomeranging. It's easy to see a smudge on your neighbor's face and be oblivious to the ugly sneer on your own. Do you have the nerve to say, "Let me wash your face for you," when your own face is distorted by contempt? It's this whole traveling road-show mentality all over again, playing a holier-than-thou part instead of just living your part. Wipe that ugly sneer off your own face, and you might be fit to offer a washcloth to your neighbor.

—MATTHEW 7:1–5 (MSG)

Day 10

INTRINSIC VALUE

Are not five sparrows sold for two cents? Yet not one of them is forgotten before God. Indeed, the very hairs of your head are all numbered. Do not fear; you are more valuable than many sparrows.

—LUKE 12:6–7 (NASB)

Pray It Through

Dear Father God, Thank You that my intrinsic value is not dependent on man's opinion. My true value is in You alone. Thank You for valuing who I am and for constantly showing me what I can be in You.

Thank You for knowing the number of hairs on my head and for knowing every intimate detail about my life. I love knowing that nothing takes You by surprise. I am loved by a king! I'm loved by the creator of the universe! I'm loved by the maker of my soul. I am loved!

You are great and mighty O Lord, my God. Yet You see fit to care about my every need. You care about the twists and turns in my life. Thank You for caring about me!

Oh yes, You shaped me first inside, then out; You formed me in my mother's womb. I thank you, High God—you're breath-taking! Body and soul, I am marvelously made! I worship in adoration—what a creation! You know me inside and out, You know every bone in my body; You know exactly how I was made, bit by bit, how I was sculpted from nothing into something. Like an open book, You watched me grow from conception to birth; all the stages of my life were spread out before you, The days of my life all prepared before I'd even lived one day.

—PSALM 139:13–16 (MSG)

Day 11

LIVING THE ABUNDANT LIFE

The thief comes only in order to steal and kill and destroy. I came that they may have and enjoy life, and have it in abundance (to the full, till it overflows).

—JOHN 10:10 (AMP)

Pray It Through

Lord, please help me to remember that my enemy is out to destroy me. He is looking for opportunities today to steal, kill, and destroy me. May I not forget that my enemy roams around like a roaring lion.

Be self-controlled and alert. Your enemy the devil prowls around like a roaring lion looking for someone to devour. Resist him, standing firm in the faith, because you know that your brothers throughout the world are undergoing the same kind of sufferings.

—1 PETER 5:8–9

Lord, please help me to be self-controlled and alert today. May I stand firm in the faith that You have given me and resist the enemy when he comes to attack.

Today, I celebrate that You have come to give me life and not just that, You came that I might experience the full and abundant life. Oh, how sweet that is! Lord, I pray that I will enjoy the fullness of life that You offer me today!

> *See how I love Your precepts; preserve my life, O LORD, according to Your love.*
>
> —PSALM 119:159

Day 12

SAFE IN GOD'S HANDS

The sheep that are My own hear and are listening to My voice; and I know them, and they follow Me. And I give them eternal life, and they shall never lose it or perish throughout the ages. [To all eternity they shall never by any means be destroyed.] And no one is able to snatch them out of My hand. My Father, Who has given them to Me, is greater and mightier than all [else]; and no one is able to snatch [them] out of the Father's hand.

—JOHN 10:27–29 (AMP)

Pray It Through

Lord, I rejoice that nothing and no one can snatch me from Your hand. What a beautiful promise You have given me to cling to. I love the fact that nothing can take me away from You. I love that You will forever be the Lord of my life. Lord, please strengthen my walk daily and help me to live more righteously before You. May my fumbles be fewer and farther between as I daily surrender myself to You and Your work.

Lord, please continue Your sanctification process in my heart. May I remember that even when the process seems hard and intense at times, that it's all worth it. You are continuing Your amazing work in me, and in that, I rejoice. Thank You for reminding me daily that "He who began a good work in me will carry it to completion until the day of Christ Jesus" (Philippians 1:6).

> *If the LORD delights in a man's way, He makes his steps firm; though he stumble, he will not fall, for the LORD upholds him with His hand.*
>
> —PSALM 37:23–24

FOR GOD'S GLORY

When he heard this, Jesus said, "This sickness will not end in death. No, it is for God's glory so that God's Son may be glorified through it." Jesus loved Martha and her sister and Lazarus. Yet when He heard that Lazarus was sick, He stayed where He was for two more days.

—JOHN 11:4–6

Pray It Through

Lord, please help me to remember that Your timing is perfect. That sometimes, the waiting is just another way to reveal who You are and bring You glory. Lord, may I find joy in the waiting, knowing that You have a purpose through it all. Please increase my faith through my current obstacle. Help me to walk by faith, not by sight (2 Corinthians 5:7). May I not lose sight of all that You can and will do through every difficult situation that I face.

Lord, please help me to honor You through my waiting time and cling to the promises I have in Your word. May I run to Your truth and find safety in the shadow of You, the almighty! May I trust in Your unfailing love, Your perfect plan, and Your beautiful work in my life.

> *And we know that in all things God works for the good of those who love Him, who have been called according to His purpose.*
>
> —ROMANS 8:28

Day 14

LIVING BY FAITH

Now on His way to Jerusalem, Jesus traveled along the border between Samaria and Galilee. As He was going into a village, ten men who had leprosy met Him. They stood at a distance and called out in a loud voice, "Jesus, Master, have pity on us!" When He saw them, He said, "Go, show yourselves to the priests." And as they went, they were cleansed.

—LUKE 17:11–14

Pray It Through

Dear Father God, I have really come to appreciate the three words as they went. It was as the ten lepers walked out their faith that they received the miracle. It was as they were going on with life that they experienced something that would forever change them. Lord, please help me to remember that life doesn't stop when things are tough. Life keeps right on going. But it's when I put feet to my faith that I see huge answers to prayer.

I need Your help to remember this! It's as I walk along in faith, living life for You, my King that I am healed, refreshed, strengthened, renewed, and ready for more! Your hand of love never stops pouring in to my life. You continue to be my steady rock in a "not-so-steady world." You are my hope when the world is hopeless. You are my strength when all I feel is weakness. You are my joy when life brings sorrow. You are my everything!

Lord, as I walk out today, please help me to remember these words.

> *Now faith is being sure of what we hope for and certain of what we do not see.*
>
> —HEBREWS 11:1

Day 15

HAVE MERCY ON ME

The Pharisee took his stand ostentatiously and began to pray thus before and with himself: God, I thank You that I am not like the rest of men—extortioners (robbers), swindlers [unrighteous in heart and life], adulterers—or even like this tax collector here. I fast twice a week; I give tithes of all that I gain. But the tax collector, [merely] standing at a distance, would not even lift up his eyes to heaven, but kept striking his breast, saying, O God, be favorable (be gracious, be merciful) to me, the especially wicked sinner that I am!

—LUKE 18:11–13 (AMP)

Pray It Through

Lord, please help me to never forget how sinful I am. May I continually compare myself to Christ and look for ways to be more Christlike. Lord, please fill me up with Yourself. I want so much of You that there's nothing left of me. Please burn my sinful nature away that I may serve You more wholeheartedly, worship You more readily, pray with great adoration, seek Your face with more urgency, humble myself before You, and display strength under control!

> *God, have mercy on me, a sinner.*
>
> —LUKE 18:13

Lord, help me to never compare myself with anyone but You, Jesus. Please have mercy on me for my sinful behavior. I pray that I will be more Christlike with every passing day, if not every hour!

Lord, I humble myself before You. May I never lift myself up, but may I only live to lift You up. Please convict me quickly when I have a judgmental or critical spirit. May I live to glorify You. May my life be honoring to You and reflect a heart changed by Your word!

> *Humble yourselves, therefore, under God's mighty hand, that He may lift you up in due time.*
>
> —1 PETER 5:6

NO COMPARISON

When those hired first came, they thought that they would receive more; but each of them also received a denarius. When they received it, they grumbled at the landowner, saying, "These last men have worked only one hour, and you have made them equal to us who have borne the burden and the scorching heat of the day." But he answered and said to one of them, 'Friend, I am doing you no wrong; did you not agree with me for a denarius? Take what is yours and go, but I wish to give to this last man the same as to you. Is it not lawful for me to do what I wish with what is my own? Or is your eye envious because I am generous?' So the last shall be first, and the first last."

—MATTHEW 20:10–16 (NASB)

Pray It Through

Dear Father God, I pray that I will not be distracted by what You do for others. May I not be jealous, and may I not covet what You give to anyone. May I rejoice in what I've been given, and may I never begrudge anyone anything.

May I not compare myself to anyone on this earth but only to Jesus! May I live fully surrendered, fully empowered, and fully abandoned to Your purpose alone! God, please have all of me. Mold me and shape me into all that You desire me to be. And please smooth away all my rough edges.

Lord, I pray that my heart will be glad when You bless those around me. I pray that I will rejoice with them in Your blessings on their life. And at the end of the day, may I not ask why didn't You do that for me, but may I say, "Thank You God for all that You have given me."

> *Envy is the art of counting the other fellow's blessings instead of your own.*
>
> —HAROLD COFFIN

> *Blessed are those who have learned to acclaim You, who walk in the light of Your presence, O LORD.*
>
> —PSALM 89:15

Day 17

FILLED WITH AWE

They were now on the way up to Jerusalem, and Jesus was walking ahead of them. The disciples were filled with awe, and the people following behind were overwhelmed with fear.

—MARK 10:32 (NLT)

READ MARK 10:32-34

Pray It Through

Lord, the closer I walk with You, the more I live in awe of You. The closer I get to You through reading the Word and applying it to my life, the more secure I feel in the steps I take. I find comfort in Your peace that passes all understanding. I find strength in the words You have written to me. I find joy in Your great faithfulness. And I find hope in all Your promises. The closer I get to You, the more my life takes on meaning and purpose.

I know that fear creeps in when I stray from Your commands. Fear comes when I misplace my time and don't give You Your rightful place in my life. Fear creeps in when I take You off the throne of my heart and place my problem there instead. Lord, fear is real, so real that it can cripple me if I do not walk in the assurance of Your Truth.

I hand all of my fears over to You. I cast every care of my heart at the foot of the cross! May I have a greater awe of You today and every day that I live!

> *Cast your burden on the Lord [releasing the weight of it] and He will sustain you; He will never allow the [consistently] righteous to be moved (made to slip, fall, or fail).*
>
> —PSALM 55:22 (AMP)

Day 18

A SERVANT'S HEART

It is not this way among you, but whoever wishes to become great among you shall be your servant, and whoever wishes to be first among you shall be your slave; just as the Son of Man did not come to be served, but to serve, and to give His life a ransom for many. —MATTHEW 20:26–28 (NASB)

Pray It Through

Lord, please teach me what it means to be Your servant. Please give me a greater sense of humility.

Lord, please give me a servant's heart. May I live to lift You up. May I glorify You with my thoughts, words, and actions. Lord, may I serve You with all that I am and become more available for You.

Please increase my awareness of times that You want to use me, and may Your Holy Spirit speak through me. I pray that I will have the mindset of Christ, always live with an eternal perspective. May my eyes be forever fixed on eternity, and may I live to hear the words, "Well, done, thy good and faithful servant."

His master replied, "Well done, good and faithful servant! You have been faithful with a few things; I will put you in charge of many things. Come and share your master's happiness!"

—MATTHEW 25:21

NO MORE GRUMBLING

When Jesus came to the place, He looked up and said to him, "Zaccheus, hurry and come down, for today I must stay at your house." And he hurried and came down and received Him gladly. When they saw it, they all began to grumble, saying, "He has gone to be the guest of a man who is a sinner."

—LUKE 19:5–7 (NASB)

Pray It Through

Dear Father God, I'm so sorry for the times I have grumbled and complained when I have watched You work in others. I'm sorry for my critical and judgmental spirit at times. Lord, I pray that You will help me to be constantly aware of my own sin and my need for Christ. May I not judge anyone around me but be thankful for the times when You are at work in others.

Lord, please help me to celebrate when You do great things for anyone I know. May I not be like the people who grumbled in this verse, but may I rejoice when someone comes home to You.

Lord, thank You for doing a tremendous work in my life even when I was undeserving of it. Thank You for never giving up on me!

> *"You see, at just the right time, when we were still powerless, Christ died for the ungodly. Very rarely will anyone die for a righteous man, though for a good man someone might possibly dare to die. But God demonstrates His own love for us in this: While we were still sinners, Christ died for us."*
>
> —ROMANS 5:6–8

Day 20

MY OFFERING

While He was in Bethany at the home of Simon the leper, and reclining at the table, there came a woman with an alabaster vial of very costly perfume of pure nard; and she broke the vial and poured it over His head. But some were indignantly remarking to one another, "Why has this perfume been wasted? For this perfume might have been sold for over three hundred denarius, and the money given to the poor." And they were scolding her. But Jesus said, "Let her alone; why do you bother her? She has done a good deed to Me. For you always have the poor with you, and whenever you wish you can do good to them; but you do not always have Me."

—MARK 14:3–7 (NASB)

Pray It Through

Lord, I pray that I will pour out my life as a constant offering for You. I pray that my heart will be so filled up with the things of You that my mouth naturally speaks only what is pleasing in Your sight. Oh Lord, may I worship You with my days. May I not take a breath without expressing extreme gratitude to You for giving it to me.

May my steps be ordered by You. May my words be used to bring You glory! May my heart be steadfast in the things of You! May my life be an offering to You. May I worship You with my moments! May You receive all the honor that You are due from me. I pray that I will live my life to honor the death Jesus died.

May I not live a single day in haste or waste. May I make the most of the moments I am given, and may I cherish every sweet day that You give me. Lord, please increase my ability to worship You. May I bring You the best of what I have today and every day!

> *Be imitators of God, therefore, as dearly loved children and live a life of love, just as Christ loved us and gave Himself up for us as a fragrant offering and sacrifice to God.*
>
> —EPHESIANS 5:1–2

Day 21

PRUNING TIME

I am the true vine, and my Father is the gardener. He cuts off every branch in me that bears no fruit, while every branch that does bear fruit He prunes so that it will be even more fruitful.

—JOHN 15:1–2

READ JOHN 15:1-17

Pray It Through

Lord, please prune any part of me that is not bearing fruit for You. May the transforming life of Christ pulsate through my very being as I cling to the nutrients found in the source of life.

Remain in me, and I will remain in you. No branch can bear fruit by itself; it must remain in the vine. Neither can you bear fruit unless you remain in Me.

—JOHN 15:4

Lord, I want to abide in You. I want to find nourishment for my soul in the life-giving nutrients that flow from Your being. May the sap of the Holy Spirit flow freely through me, and may I bear fruit for You!

I am the vine; you are the branches. If a man remains in Me and I in him, he will bear much fruit; apart from Me you can do nothing.

—JOHN 15:5

I can't do anything without You, Lord! It's so important for me to steal away as many moments as I can with You throughout my day. I know that nothing in my life will be well done without the power that comes from waiting on You and seeking Your purpose through it.

Lord, today I feast upon the truth I find in Your Word. May Your words be stitched into the very fiber of my being that I may live out my days for Your purpose. Lord, today is Yours. May I live it out in a way that honors You alone!

If you remain in Me and My words remain in you, ask whatever you wish, and it will be given you.

—JOHN 15:7

Day 22

RIGHTEOUS ANGER

On reaching Jerusalem, Jesus entered the temple area and began driving out those who were buying and selling there. He overturned the tables of the money changers and the benches of those selling doves, and would not allow anyone to carry merchandise through the temple courts.

—MARK 11:15–16

Pray It Through

Lord, please help me to remember not to sin in my anger. I see that You had a righteous anger as You saw people mistreat the temple. Lord, I pray that my anger will not be spurred by personal insults, rejection, petty frustrations, or minor irritations.

Lord, I pray that I will rise above the things that frustrate me. May I keep my eyes fixed on You! May I be more concerned about You and how You are represented in my life! I pray that I will take every thought captive and make it obedient to Christ. May I not let my thoughts run away from me. Lord, may I honor You with my emotions today!

In your anger do not sin: Do not let the sun go down while you are still angry.

—EPHESIANS 4:26

MY RESPONSIBILITY

Even after Jesus had done all these miraculous signs in their presence, they still would not believe in Him. This was to fulfill the word of Isaiah the prophet: "Lord, who has believed our message and to whom has the arm of the Lord been revealed?"

—JOHN 12:37–38

Pray It Through

Lord, please help me to remember that my responsibility is to be a witness for You, to share the light of the gospel through my words and actions. I can't force anyone to believe in You. May I just walk out my days for You and live to make You known through every step I take.

Yet at the same time many even among the leaders believed in Him. But because of the Pharisees they would not confess their faith for fear they would be put out of the synagogue; for they loved praise from men more than praise from God.

—JOHN 12:42–43

Lord, please help me to always be more concerned about what You think and not what those around me think. May I live to lift You up!

> *The fear of human opinion disables; trusting in GOD protects you from that.*
>
> —PROVERBS 29:25 (MSG)

Day 24

A FORGIVING HEART

And when you stand praying, if you hold anything against anyone, forgive him, so that your Father in heaven may forgive you your sins.

—MARK 11:25

Pray It Through

Lord, I come humbly before You asking You to search my heart. Please show me where I have been unforgiving toward others. Please show me where I have been holding a hurt and where resentment has built up in my heart.

Lord, I don't want any unforgiveness in my life. I don't want anything in my life that would keep me from fully serving You. Lord, I know that an unforgiving spirit can keep me from fully experiencing Your work in my life, so please help me to recognize when my heart is holding resentment. Please help me to live in forgiveness toward others, knowing how much I have been forgiven because of the cross.

May resentment, bitterness, hatred, unforgiveness, and criticalness be banned from my life. Lord, help me to recognize when my heart is not fully surrendered to You and when I have placed my emotions above Your goodness.

> *Search me, O God, and know my heart; test me and know my anxious thoughts. See if there is any offensive way in me, and lead me in the way everlasting.*
>
> PSALM 139:23–24

Day 25

HOLY SPIRIT DUCT TAPE

They were unable to trap Him in what He said there in public. And astonished by His answer, they became silent.

—LUKE 20:26

Pray It Through

Lord, please teach me to respond quickly to others in love. May I not be trapped by words, but may I recognize the motivation behind them. Please increase my wisdom that I may respond wisely to others. I pray that my heart will be flooded with Your joy, peace, and love so that out of the overflow of it, my mouth speaks only what edifies You!

Let no unwholesome word proceed from your mouth, but only such a word as is good for edification according to the need of the moment, so that it will give grace to those who hear.

—EPHESIANS 4:29 (NASB)

Lord, please put Your Holy Spirit duct tape over my mouth, and help me keep better control of the words I say. Please help me to be more conscious of the words that proceed from my mouth, and may I only say what edifies the body of Christ.

> *When words are many, sin is not absent, but he who holds his tongue is wise.*
>
> —PROVERBS 10:19

Lord, help me to keep my words few so that I can be counted among those who are wise. Help me to remember that I'm bound to sin the more I speak. Please help me to have better control over my tongue and to make my words count.

> *May the words of my mouth and the meditation of my heart be pleasing in Your sight, O LORD, my Rock and my Redeemer.*
>
> —PSALM 19:14

OVERWHELMED

Then He said to them, "My soul is overwhelmed with sorrow to the point of death. Stay here and keep watch with Me."

—MATTHEW 26:38

Pray It Through

Lord, I can't begin to imagine how overwhelming the thought of the cross, the separation from the Father, and the weight of our sins were. Lord, thank You for not giving in to how You felt that day. Thank You for moving forward even when the weight of the world was on Your shoulders.

Going a little farther, He fell with his face to the ground and prayed, "My Father, if it is possible, may this cup be taken from Me. Yet not as I will, but as You will."

—MATTHEW 26:39

Lord, may I follow Your lead. May this be my prayer as I daily surrender myself to the work of Your hands. May I not seek to have my will accomplished, but may I seek to accomplish Your will!

And being in anguish, He prayed more earnestly, and His sweat was like drops of blood falling to the ground.

—LUKE 22:44

Lord, I cannot fully imagine the anguish You faced. Lord, please help me to never forget what You felt and how You moved on from there. Please help me to not give in to the moments in my life when I feel blah. May I press in as You pressed in and seek to fulfill my Father's purpose, even when it hurts.

When they hurled their insults at Him, He did not retaliate; when He suffered, He made no threats. Instead, He entrusted Himself to Him who judges justly.

—1 PETER 2:23

ACT OF COMPASSION

When those who were around Him saw what was going to happen, they said, "Lord, shall we strike with the sword?" And one of them struck the slave of the high priest and cut off his right ear. But Jesus answered and said, "Stop! No more of this." And He touched his ear and healed him.

—LUKE 22:49–51 (NASB)

Pray It Through

Lord, it is so impressive to see this act of compassion toward one of Your capturers. You displayed a tremendous act of kindness during a very difficult time. You were betrayed by one of Your own disciples, arrested, and on Your way to face six trials, which would ultimately lead to Your sentence of crucifixion, You were about to take on the sins of the world, and all Your disciples deserted You. Yet You stopped to show compassion. You stopped to perform a miracle for someone who didn't deserve it. You stopped to redirect the thoughts of those around You, and You stopped to show the glory of God!

Lord, so often when I'm going through something difficult, I have a low tolerance for others. I do not show compassion as readily as I should when my heart is aching.

Lord, I pray that I will be more like Christ and show compassion to others even in the midst of my own pain. May I not miss a moment of what You have for me, Lord! Please help me to direct my thoughts and my actions toward You! May I better reflect the mindset of Christ that I see in these verses.

Your attitude should be the same as that of Christ Jesus.

—PHILIPPIANS 2:5

Day 28

FORGIVENESS MATTERS

Two other men, both criminals, were also led out with Him to be executed. When they came to the place called the Skull, there they crucified Him, along with the criminals—one on His right, the other on His left. Jesus said, "Father, forgive them, for they do not know what they are doing."

—LUKE 23:32–34

Pray It Through

Dear Father God, I am humbled by Jesus' first words from the cross. He was beaten beyond recognition, flogged numerous times, crowned with a crown of thorns, and received nonstop insults from those who were watching. He barely had any life left in Him. Yet His very first words from the cross were, "Father, forgive them."

Lord, I'm so sorry for the times that I have held unforgiveness in my heart toward others. Please forgive me for being insensitive, unkind, and having an unforgiving heart. I pray that You will give me the ability to forgive as quickly as Christ did from the cross.

Lord, I also see that Jesus never breathed a murmur or sigh of complaint while He faced His execution. He never waved a flag of surrender. He never once "threw in the towel." He climbed Calvary's Hill for me. My sins nailed Him to that cross. Lord, may I live every day of my life thankful for the sacrifice that was made on my behalf. May my life declare the praises of my Redeemer, and may I daily look for opportunities to raise His banner high!

Praise be to the God and Father of our Lord Jesus Christ! In His great mercy He has given us new birth into a living hope through the resurrection of Jesus Christ from the dead and into an inheritance that can never perish, spoil or fade—kept in heaven for you.

—1 PETER 1:3–4

JESUS IS RISEN

The angel said to the women, "Do not be afraid, for I know that you are looking for Jesus, who was crucified. He is not here; He has risen, just as He said. Come and see the place where He lay."

—MATTHEW 28:5–6

Pray It Through

Lord, the greatest three words ever written in history are, "He is risen!" It's because of these three words that I can now experience life. I have victory over death because You took on the grave for me. You faced death for me and conquered it! My sin held me captive. My life was headed nowhere, but You stepped in and saved me.

Satan thought he had won. I'm sure he was throwing a party as You laid in that grave for three days. But his party was interrupted as the stone was rolled away and the angel declared, "He is not here. He has risen, just as He said" (Matthew 28:6). Wow, I love those words, Lord. Just as You said! That is so important for me to remember.

You always come through on Your promises. You promised to conquer death, and You did. You promise to give me life to the full, and You do. You promise that my home is not here! You promise that I have a place of no pain or sorrow awaiting me. Heaven will be my eternal destination. Heaven will be my final resting place. All because of three words, "He is risen." My Lord has risen from the grave. Death could not hold Him captive. He is alive! My Redeemer lives!

> *Could it be any clearer? Our old way of life was nailed to the cross with Christ, a decisive end to that sin-miserable life—no longer at sin's every beck and call! What we believe is this: If we get included in Christ's sin-conquering death, we also get included in his life-saving resurrection. We know that when Jesus was raised from the dead it was a signal of the end of death-as-the-end. Never again will death have the last word. When Jesus died, He took sin down with Him, but alive He brings God down to us. From now on, think of it this way: Sin speaks a dead language that means nothing to you; God speaks your mother tongue, and you hang on every word. You are dead to sin and alive to God. That's what Jesus did.*
>
> —ROMANS 6:8-11 (MSG)

Day 30

AS I GO

Then Jesus came to them and said, "All authority in heaven and on earth has been given to Me. Therefore go and make disciples of all nations, baptizing them in the name of the Father and of the Son and of the Holy Spirit, and teaching them to obey everything I have commanded you. And surely I am with you always to the very end of the age."

—MATTHEW 28:18-20

Pray It Through

Lord, thank You for this instruction on how to live my life until Your return. Lord, please help me to actively disciple others. As I walk through life, may I be aware of the opportunities around me to shine the light of Jesus. May I be ready to give an answer for the hope that I have to anyone who asks me.

But in your hearts set apart Christ as Lord. Always be prepared to give an answer to everyone who asks you to give the reason for the hope that you have. But do this with gentleness and respect.

—1 PETER 3:15

Lord, may I daily pursue You and Your mission. Please help me to teach others how to follow You, how to obey You, and how to live out Your word. May Your truth be my guide! May my passion for the lost be increased daily. May I serve You to the best of my ability. Lord, I want to be used to bring others in to the saving knowledge of Jesus Christ. I pray that I will be a living testimony for Your glory. May the opportunities that exist around me to spread the gospel not be wasted or squandered. May my mouth open only to bring You praise! May my heart declare Your goodness, and may those around me see the hope of Jesus in me.

I'm all Yours, Lord! I'm ready to be used by You! As I go today, may I serve You in every possible way. May my hands reach out to love someone who is hurting, may my feet go where the gospel has not reached, and may my mouth declare the praises of You, my King!

For it is by grace you have been saved, through faith–and this not from yourselves, it is the gift of God–not by works, so that no one can boast. For we are God's workmanship, created in Christ Jesus to do good works, which God prepared in advance for us to do.

—EPHESIANS 2:8–10

BIBLIOGRAPHY

"Harold Coffin Quotes." Think Exist. Accessed September 10, 2014

Pentecost, J. Dwight, and John Danilson. *The Words and Works of Jesus Christ: A Study of the Life of Christ*. Grand Rapids, Mich.: Zondervan Pub. House, 1981.

"Words, Words, Words…Quotes." Quotes: Words, Speech and Talk. Accessed September 22, 2014. http://www. tentmaker.org/ Quotes/wordsquotes.htm.

I write these things to you
who **BELIEVE** in the **name**
of the **Son of God** so that
you may **KNOW** that you have
ETERNAL LIFE.
This is the **confidence** we have
in approaching **God**: that if we
ask **anything** according to
His *will*, He *hears us.*
And if we **KNOW** that
He *hears us*, whatever we ask,
we **KNOW** that we have what
we asked of **Him.**

....

1 JOHN 5:13-15

ABOUT THE MINISTRY

Sarah Malanowski is the Founder of a ministry called ***The Priceless Journey***. This ministry exists to empower women who have been marginalized, exploited, neglected, and abused. Sarah works diligently with a team to create resources that go into the hands of the broken all over our communities. She has a strong passion to see every woman embrace her journey of freedom and become all that God desires her to be. We encourage you to get these resources and share them with the broken in your community because every woman deserves to know that she is truly priceless.

Here are helpful resources that Sarah and her team have developed.

*You are Priceless (*English, Spanish & Chinese)
Every woman deserves to know that she is priceless. In this booklet read the testimonies of five women, who had a life-transforming encounter with Jesus Christ.

You are an Overcomer—Do you know someone struggling with depression, discouragement, thoughts of suicide, addiction, or domestic abuse? Learn what it means to overcome!

You are Fearless—Do you know anyone who feels trapped? This booklet is extremely helpful for those in the commercial sex industry and victims of human trafficking.

You are Worthy—In this booklet women will learn that being worthy is not based on what they've done but on who they already are. This booklet is especially useful in the Pregnancy Care Centers.

You are Loved—Women everywhere have the desire to be loved whether it's in the pew, the prison, the clubs, or streets. In this booklet you discover the truth is that no one can love you like God.

You are Free—Many women are caught in an endless loop of lies with little awareness that there is something more. In this booklet you will learn that Jesus will set you free! You are not your past.

You are Enough—The message of being enough is embedded—am I strong enough, beautiful enough, smart enough? The truth is these are all masks to hide the real you.

Other resources created by Sarah Malanowski are:

Make Your Moments Count—The gift of motherhood is beautiful yet crazy and exhausting. In this book 20 moms join Sarah to share their adventures and provide encouragement.

Life's Compass for Eternal Treasure—In this book Sarah unpacks Psalm 37 and shows how and where we gain direction for life. Study guide included.

All resources are available at **thepricelessjourney.org**

Victorious Mindset—In this book, you will unpack the secret of living victorious for Jesus. Every battle starts in the mind and you can overcome it with the Truth of God's Word! Sarah includes quotes from spiritual giants to remind you that you are not alone in this journey!

Infused with Joy—Being a leader is a daunting task and often filled with great demand and little reward. Be encouraged and empowered as you read this booklet designed for those in leadership.

The Priceless Journey now has an app available on both Apple and Android! Simply search Priceless Journey to find it. More features will be added soon, but for now, it's a great resource with all our booklets and more to come.

IPHONE

ANDROID

Then **Jesus** told
His disciples a
parable to show
them that they should
always **PRAY**
and **not give up.**

****

LUKE 18:1

ABOUT THE AUTHOR

Sarah is an *Amazon Bestselling Author*, Certified Life Coach, Speaker, and Founder of the nonprofit **The Priceless Journey**. She is passionate about helping people break free from limiting beliefs and life circumstances that keep them stuck, and step into lives marked by purpose, freedom, and transformation.

With over 25 years of experience in ministry and leadership, Sarah has coached and mentored hundreds of individuals from all walks of life—including leaders, parents, students, those in shelters, and individuals impacted by incarceration. Her approach is rooted in truth, compassion, and practical guidance, helping people move forward with clarity and confidence through every season of life.

Sarah's work focuses on empowering individuals to know the heart of God for themselves, heal from the past, and embrace the future God has prepared for them. She reaches people through one-on-one coaching, conferences, retreats, and group gatherings, sharing a message of hope, healing, and lasting change through the Gospel of Jesus Christ.

Looking for a Speaker?

Sarah has a way with words. Many audiences have left sharing the impact of her words and how its inspired their freedom journey. Sarah shares from the overflow of the work God has done in her life and invites you into her storyline. She loves talking about Jesus and the abundant life He promises us in John 10:10. When you're looking for a speaker to empower your group in their freedom journey, contact Sarah.

Hope@ThePricelessJourney.org | 833.691.4673 ext. 3

www.ingramcontent.com/pod-product-compliance
Ingram Content Group UK Ltd.
Pitfield, Milton Keynes, MK11 3LW, UK
UKHW020223250726
13967UKWH00001B/157